CANOODLERS

CANOODLERS

ANDREA BENNETT

NIGHTWOOD EDITIONS 2014

Nightwood Editions
P.O. Box 1779
Gibsons, BC VON 1V0
Canada
www.nightwoodeditions.com

TYPOGRAPHY & COVER DESIGN: Carleton Wilson

THE CANADA COUNCIL | LE CONSEIL DES ARTS
FOR THE ARTS | DU CANADA
SINCE 1957 | DEPUIS 1957

BRITISH COLUMBIA
ARTS COUNCIL
An agency of the Province of British Columbia

Nightwood Editions acknowledges financial support from the Government of Canada through the Canada Book Fund and the Canada Council for the Arts, and from the Province of British Columbia through the British Columbia Arts Council and the Book Publisher's Tax Credit.

This book has been produced on 100% post-consumer recycled, ancient-forest-free paper, processed chlorine-free and printed with vegetable-based dyes.

Printed and bound in Canada.

LIBRARY AND ARCHIVES CANADA CATALOGUING IN PUBLICATION

Bennett, Andrea (Andrea Kathleen), author
Canoodlers / Andrea Bennett.

Poems.
ISBN 978-0-88971-297-3 (pbk.)

I. Title.

PS8603.E5593C35 2014   C811'.6   C2014-900625-X

For Nik and Trevor Bennett

CONTENTS

Epigraph

You have a poetic sensibility,
my father says. Maybe,
when you clean your room,
you will find it.

When you are famous,

everything you do is famous. Your colonic is famous when you are famous, not to mention your facial hair, and the name of the dog or the child you are carrying. When you are famous, your living room has been staged by *House & Home*. If a hot mess reclines on the chaise and a handsome wreck answers a phone call, it is plot development.

Even if your famous house is located at the end of a private road, people will find it—will take photos that mimic screencaps from your scenes and credits. Your famous house will be Google-mapped for the best vistas.

If a handsome wreck and a hot mess walk the red carpet of their living room, it could be news. If a hot mess and a handsome wreck do morning yoga on their balcony, it is definitely news. When you are famous, you stage yourself for house and home.

There's a story

and it happens when I am twelve. There's the back seat of a car, where my best friend Jane is sitting—I can see her in the rearview. Outside it's a zoo, according to my mum. Rolling through downtown Hamilton, she says, *Some of these people truly belong in cages.* She points out the driver's side window, flicks her fingers at a woman walking. *Wouldja look at that,* she says, and so I look—crunchy blonde hair, crop top, too-short cut-offs.

Then I say one of those things that emerges from your mouth like a just-born giraffe learning to walk immediately on whatever legs it's got. *It's just a hop and skip,* I say to my mum, *between you and her.*

In the rearview, a hyena. To my left, a lioness stalking, deciding if now is the time to pounce. That's the thing, I say to myself. The thing about cages. I get it now.

Dad

We left the house wearing backpacks, took a route that skirted
the suburbs across the road from our house. The trail
dipped and rose onto hills like overturned tortoise shells.
Hear that? he asked. The name of a bird would follow:
cardinal, wren, jay, gnatcatcher, finch.
Read the landscapes. See the glaciers.
I trailed his bobbing green backpack.

He handed me his binoculars, saying *Osprey* or *Turkey vulture,*
Don't fuck with the lenses.

We wound through the valley, down the trail
beside a creek skimming grey-brown stones.
And then we climbed.
Seeing the other side of the valley, where we'd end up,
was like taking a long, deep breath. Eventually
we got to the peak, where we could see
the whole town. The middle
school with separate entrances for girls and boys,
Mike's Sports Bar, the town arena.

Ploughman's lunch, he said, unzipping the backpack
to pull out a loaf of French bread, two different kinds
of cheese. He shook his keys free and found his pocket knife,
sliced the cheese, pointed at more turkey vultures.

They're kettling, he said. *They follow drafts of air.*
Follow each other in circles, surveying the trees,
the town, the brush below them.

I'm looking for the blue-foiled eggs in the dry grasses, muddying a pair of woollen mitts. No one is shy at the Easter egg hunt. We're running from spot to spot, crouching down the steep hill near the cemetery; usually we hold our breath.

I haven't seen my mum in a while, so I find her. See Bubba the skate sharpener first, then my mum's hand on his stretched-out arm. She laughs—her hip swings close, touches his hip.

See him see me, before looking at the ground and away.

Bubba's holding two salty hot chocolates, and he gives me one as a consolation prize. He's gotta line up to get another one, so my mum takes my hand and off we go, in search of more eggs.

Dock Shoes

After he marries a pleasant single mother,
Larry the lech moves in two doors down.

One sunny day I go down to the backyard
to pick mint for tea. Rest my hand on the latch.

See my mother, gardening in cut-offs
and a sports bra, fists of dirt clinging to her knees.

Lecherous Larry leans over his wooden fence.
Lite beer in one hand, the other hand hidden.

His eyes on the hose in her hand,
her thumb on the spout.

Later, I will be scolded for not saying hello.

Later still, lecherous Larry will enter our quiet house
during a street party. He'll shimmy

out of dock shoes, pad down the hall
with bare feet. Drunk, he will look for my mother.

There's another story

my mum tells about my stepbrother's truck hitting her wooden plank fence. *He left the brake off,* she says. *That dummy.* The planks bear in now, as if eager for a game of red rover.

They used to drink at the Air Force Club, my mum and stepfather, and I'd walk over to get them when I was done work. *Let me drive,* I'd say. *I need to practise.*

Sometimes mum would say, *No, I'm driving.*

When my mum tells the story of the fence, she *tsks.* Sometimes she forgets and tells it in front of my stepbrother, that dummy.

And maybe my stepbrother's truck is an automatic. Maybe lots of people slide into the ditch on winter nights, coming home from the Air Force Club. Not able to see the clothesline, the stiff row of shoulder.

Summer

is the well-meaning guest late to the potluck, needing to use the oven for a sec. The anemics swoon, stick their feet out the windows. Deficient in iron, rich in quiet time, they think of those they think of often but never remember to call. *I am baking*, says summer, echo the anemics. *I am making you a pudding cake.* I am pitting cherries and leaving their plump cups face up, waiting for syrup.

Float

I tell Jane the guy in the spot beside us is camping alone—that it took him five minutes to put up his A-frame. *Yeah*, she says. *He sure did pitch his tent.*

Our feet punch a rhythm on the boardwalk, kick wood chips back at the squidgy ground. It smells like cedar, like the still water of Cyprus Lake, like bacon cooking in cast iron. I want to shush her—*What if he can hear?*—but blush, duck my head instead.

A crow hops along, a little ways away—flutters and resettles as Jane snaps her towel.

Our plan is to get to the middle of the stale shallow lake, float on our backs like toddlers just learning to swim. First one to fall from the float and start treading water loses.

Singing Sands

Jane and I eat miniature marshmallows
from the bag. Twenty minutes
down the road, a wetland crowded,
condensed as milk. Pitcher plants
down moths and mosquitoes

as we roast spiderdogs, popping pink
and turquoise jet-puffeds
into our impatient mouths.

at my five, six, seven—one, two, three o'clock as I pump and boil water from the bay. A charcoal filter, a small flame, a pouch of coffee suspended from a stick. Don't the loons know

we've coined them already? The cove opens like an ear, hardscrabble rocks along the lobe. At night, I keep thinking *bear*. Pee on my kite-shaped tent; hitch the food, soap, deodorant up a branch that sags from the weight.

The cove is an ear and swimming is drinking from the faucet. There is nothing more to be said.

I swim out from the shore until I am warm—practise a dolphin kick. Pretend I am a quiet myth, arching and surfacing where no one can see me.

A Wig, a Watch, a Convertible

The gap between her teeth is a rabbit hole
with two lips blooming top and bottom.

Or it is like vertigo—a figure
falling, another in a scarf.

There are potions for shrinking and growing.
A wig. A watch. A convertible.

Jimmy Stewart and a rabbit. A bell tower,
a hole.

A suitcase full of clothing. Petticoats
and Mary Janes. A fall, a fall.

A jungle gym, a taut wire

of crows, pumps, pencil skirts. Not a hair

out of place. Lovebirds under a blanket.
An open flue. Lipstick

swatch of blood at Melanie's hairline,
at Mitch's wrist.

Convertible open
as a stone-blue eye, pedal to the floor.

The lovebirds, quiet.

The ornithologist saying, *Birds*
of different species don't flock together.

Gulls cracking windows like crème brûlée.

Later: diner patrons, perched in a row.

Melanie slapping the mother who says, *The trouble—*
it only started when you came.

Christmas

happens when a solitary child builds a snow fort in his front yard. At first there is excitement. All of the snow from the yard can be mobilized without guilt. The months ahead are pack ice, firn, promises; no one thinks about grass.

Christmas gets built closest to the street, where everyone can see and be seen, whether they are walking a dog or parking a car or lighting a menorah. After building Christmas, though, the child must crawl inside of it.

Doubts are like graves, out of sight in a snow fort. The child might remember an urban legend: a boy hiding in leaves on his own lawn, unseen, found unwittingly by his father's lawnmower.

Like a Vacation

My mum asks, *D'you know what I mean? Can you pass the pepper? He's not allowed to have salt. Oh, and the gravy.*

Grace, says my stepfather Randy. *We should do grace.* Like it's a vacation, I think.

Dad, says Randy, *why don't you say grace?* And Poppa pups his lips, giggles, tells us a story about his cats. He has six cats. No, eight. We should do Greece, I think, thinking of the dish of roast potatoes. And then I think: you don't want to be here. You: brother, stepbrothers, significant others. Assembled parents, you don't want to be here in your own house. There's a sister missing; she's defected.

Dearly beloved, we have tabled our concerns at this table. We are peppering them into conversation. Dearly beloved, Don Cherry has better conversation skills than my stepfather, and my mother doesn't love me anymore.

A bird on the beach in Sarasota

snaps its beak shut—the clasp of an elegant clutch. It's a tern, toeing its way through the red drift. And two men are walking the beach, legs thin as gulls.

Nana turns to watch a boat being lowered into the harbour. *I'll bet you they're going fishing,* she says.

Another man clears his throat and reaches for his cooler—lounger keeling starboard. *Thirsty?* he asks the woman beside him. *Want a Busch?* The cooler is the kind where you push a button and the lid slides back.

Later, my nana and I will watch the news and they'll pan a beach, saying *epidemic* and *heart problem.* Filming people from the neck down, walking—or lounging, belly up. *Portion sizes.*

What do you fancy for supper? asks Nana. I watch the tern pecking, pulling threads from its patch of seaweed. *I don't know,* I answer. *I don't really care.* And she clucks and says, *The wind's picked up—we'd better get going.* She folds up her chair. *Not a blummin' pelican,* she says. *I can't believe it. Not a one.*

We leave the beach, drive away in a sand-coloured Toyota. I press my face to the window glass. See the gull-legged man visiting the man with the Busch—clearing his empties. See that news shot of torsos torquing, feet grubbing their ways through the sand.

All You Need to Know About Gators

Florida is the only place in the world for alligators and crocodiles together. Here, visiting my nana, I need to visit the alligators. *Oh no, says my nana, you don't want to do that.* Although I print out a fact sheet—only three people bitten in the whole history of the park— Nana can't bear the thought.

My mum phones my nana every night while I'm visiting. Every night the same: my mother's mouth in the chamber of a fluted glass. I tell her about the alligator plan, and she says, *Hunh. Ha! Let me tell you, I'll tell you that's just not gonna fly.*

After we hang up, I tell my nana that I don't feel like I know my mum at all. Can you tell me something about her? Who she dated, what she wanted to do with her life? *I guess it's been a while since you lived with her,* says my nana. *She was a sweet kid. She dated a neighbour, Tom or Tim, or maybe they were close friends.*

My aunt calls and I go to the fridge. A third of a bottle of Zinfandel, a halfer of Chardonnay. While my aunt worries my nana—her trip to the airport to get me, the wind chilling through her slacks—I thumb the edge of the fact sheet. *All You Need to Know About Gators.* I drink all the alcohol in the house.

entered my kitchen. He stood over the failed pot of yogurt and said decisively, *The culture is not strong enough.*

I tried to tell him my mother never made yogurt (my father didn't either), but he'd gone.

I put another pot in a warm bath, set it in a spot not too hot or cold. Addressing an audience filled with ancestors, I said, *The trick is to start with a good yogurt and whisk a bit into the milk when it reaches room temperature.*

After the second pot failed, I put myself into a warm bath. Adorno sat on the toilet seat, watching my breasts float at the surface.

He did not say anything as my skin blushed with heat, kept quiet when the bath cooled, did nothing but watch as my nipples hardened from pride or chill.

Eighteen

I.

Eighteen. A job
my mum got for me
at Hamilton Parks & Rec. The park
a park only if you were being generous
like my nana is generous:
please eat these cookies,
can I get you a cup of tea with milk?

US Steel in the middle distance.

One other girl on my shift.
She said, *I am bisexual.*
I did not say, *Me too.*

We were in the cinderblock
bathrooms, she was holding
a concrete drill.

My boyfriend says it's not cheating
if it's with girls.

We stripped flaking
salmon-grey paint from the walls—
better contact point.

I hadn't slept in days.
Drill heavy
as the waves of Lake Ontario.

A yearling gull outside
calling for its mum
or a friend
or food.

You try, she said,
so I did—
tip of the drill against
the concrete, boring
a small hole, and
then a widening one.

II.

Walked the rail trail
from Hamilton to Dundas
bars of Hess Village
home to Hillsdale Court
still in my steel-toes.

Sky murky, red.

Threw up
near a stand of sumac
behind the A&P.

Home in time
to head right back
out to work.

III.

Three of us
in a chained-off
field of brush
and loosestrife.

Each to our own
riding mower,
eye to the ground for
bottles, needles.

Brush is grass
and sky is up:
narrating myself
like the world
was a picture book.

On the way back out,
I couldn't remember
how we made it
under the chain.

So I held it up,
idled till the others
were through.

Then, me.

Front of the mower
bucking the difference
between ground and sky.

Cracked yellow
chain guard crushing
its air filter.

IV.

Reckoning.

Lied to the boss
when he lined us up
in front of the mowers.

Two days later,
bitten by a spider
that was never supposed to get
as far north as the Hammer.

Pulling into traffic
five days after that,
I didn't see a speeding car.

Hubcap actually rolling
through the intersection.

My boyfriend never said
it wasn't cheating
if it was with girls.

The waves of Lake Ontario
heavy as a drill.

A twenty-sixer
of my father's whiskey,
twelve and a half
little pills.

An ambulance,
the hospital.

If you did something evil,

it would burn red and hot, like cranking the wrong element all the way to max. A pot of water would watch, cold, beside the wrong coiled red spring. The wrong element wanting the comfort of the weight of the pot. One thing needlessly hot while everything else stayed cold. A hand hovering, a face blistering in even, semi-circular lines.

Because the Juices Run Pink

Because the cords are tangled. Because the downstairs neighbours are watching an action movie. Because you can feel it in your empty stomach. Because everyone else is at drag queen bingo, drinking cheap doubles. Because you are at home, deciding if you can go home for the holidays. Because your mother forgets that you called. Because you are working, but not quite enough. Because you are working too much. Because you are an appetite. Because you take the organs and the neck out of the bird before it goes in the oven. Because no one has called you. Because you forgot to call, or your call has been forgotten. Because decisions need to be made. Because of saturation points. Because of satiation. Because you have to open yourself up, expose your organs to a hand. Because eventually the juices run clear.

Toby

is the name my nana gave this dog. At my stepsister's wedding (the one who defected), my mother laces her arms around my neck and says, *I think you'll like the video Randy took.* This is the first time I've seen my mother in years, the first words between us.

Toby is the kind of dog who'll one day weep red silt down the white fur of his jowls. Who looks like a sad stuffed bear, cradled by mother. She says, *I am teaching him how to swim.*

I couldn't have come up with anything better, says my nana, *for your mother. You should see him. Such a dear. Her own little dear.*

In #2K11,

My mum defriends me on Facebook, and this means I am cut out of the family.

The Sky Is Winning

The insects are supposed to take over the world. Despite the easy crunch of a potato bug or the way a centipede goes off like a half-hearted firework. Despite beetles cracking open like walnuts at Christmastime. Sheer numbers. The rest of us, sheared off. Them: puffing and popping and crunching like Cracker Jacks.

Cracker Jack this: a few left over and they'd repopulate. Some nestled under the sternums of you or me, sheared off. No reason to be mad, because we are dead. Be comforted by the thought of things climbing and crawling and hatching after all the mammals have burst their fragile little hearts.

What would your ventricles have to say if the sky started winning? I wouldn't picture a giant vacuum, schlumping it all cloudward. Would you think: nothing in grade eleven physics prepared me for this? Would the thought rattle around like a marble sent through the central vac? Would you wonder what would become of the cockroaches—if everything we'd ever learned about the cockroaches was just a lie, after all?

The man who was a high bird

was my friend. He was an albatross, I'm sure, though I've only seen one at the ROM in the same flight over and over, on the same lines from the ceiling—unless maybe it sometimes comes down.

My friend had the type of jaw you could cup your hands onto. You could make a heart with your two hands and two thumbs and you could lean in toward him.

Talons

I told her the story of
the owl perched in the corner of my room—
how it flew away, eventually.
What kind of owl? she asked.

My thumbs met my indexes
to draw loops around my eyes.
Snowy, I told her.

We kept the heat low
the winter it came,
stocked the cupboards
with stacks of potatoes and mice.

She said she'd play the part of the owl
now, if I wanted.
And though her eyes opened
like a blade unsheathing, she kept
her nails so short they flashed
a slip of pink skin.

Beaches

She and I talk about home like it's the first pair of underwear you picked out for yourself. Didn't pinch, developed holes, etc. Home is the first place you live without your parents, we decide, because we are like that.

Her boyfriend is mop-headed, grins like a kid with a bucket and spade. Sometimes she's the beach and sometimes she's the mum, saying *Sunscreen, fer chrissakes, sunscreen.* I prefer to say partner, have also heard sweetheart. Dunno, yet, if I have a partner or a sweetheart or what. *You've stuck your legs out one side of the umbrella,* she says, *and stayed mostly in the shade.* She cracks a joke about fish aplenty.

What we are going to do with our lives: work with our hands. The way people who think about home as underwear work with their hands. The way they always go home. And what of our loves? Well, we'll write poetry the way fishmongers write poetry, knifing a steelhead open like a cherished book.

A Week in the House of What Repute

Eight people in a house with five bedrooms—a kitchen up, a kitchen down. The glasses are dirty so we go the Elks Den, our local at the bottom of the road. It's full of locals. One who is psychic says I'm with child, with Karl's child, but no I'm with Beauchamp who's sharking at pool though he's an otter.

The locals don't like it, don't like him. A fight breaks out—what can we do but leave for our house of dirties, our house of empties. Bartender flipping a lid, Beauchamp flipping a coin. He meets Karl and me at home with a bottle of peach schnapps. Tucks it in his coat, tucks himself beside me, holds my hand and drifts circular in sleep.

In the morning, circles on Natalie's toast. I sing a song about her fried eggs, she reads the DSM-IV.

All the glasses are dirty, Sarah is mad all the glasses are dirty. I say I'll clean them, task the boys to the bathrooms. We need to muck it all out—there's school to go to and probably work.

I could tell you all the things I am to the DSM-IV. I could tell you the song I sang.

Beauchamp adds a Schlitz to the Schlitz pyramid, Karl narrates a bowel movement. Karl and Natalie decide to get married—to get *friend married*, wind their souls together in friendship forever.

*

Beauchamp hauls a two-four home on the bus. Sits near the back, near two men talking about work at the slaughterhouse near our house. I wake up with visions, the one says; the other says I got meds for that. I keep seeing everything as meat, the one says, and the other says there's nothing you can do about the blood in the seams of your boots—on the kill floor, blood to your ankles or more. That night, we hear animals on the wind.

*

Neal gets a job at Better Beef. Guess where the veggie burgers are packed, he says, same place as the beef. Leaves for the night shift. We stay hungry, take a couple grams, get kitted out for Karl and Natalie. Fire in the backyard. Two friends from out of town show up—surprise. I try to write my number down but it turns into a wolf.

The night is a wolf. Sarah's fur stole, Karl's veil, Natalie's sheath of shawls. People ride bikes right down the stairs, right into the basement. Anyone else want to get married?

We are gathered here for this Karl and this Natalie. Beauchamp will join this Karl and this Natalie. A procession, a blown bass amp—the sound of a heart pumping. We proceed. You may now kiss your Karl. Peach schnapps. May I kiss your Karl? We know the drop ceiling, we know the tile floor.

*

The bed is a raft in the middle of the room. We float like otters, slick and furry. The woman from the local wasn't psychic with my child. It is hard to get the blood from the seams, it is hard to clean the animal from my hands.

Neal comes home, says it's time to muck it out. All the glasses are dirty, all the bottles are empty. The night is a wolf, the day is. Sarah lights the element. Sarah wants Neal in bed. It's easier in bed, drifting in circles.

Five bedrooms for eight people. There's school to get to and probably work.

Jane & Anna

Anna's moved back to our hometown. She drifts behind the bar. The punks say she has a voice like roadkill. *Dead-Panna.*

Jane is a colour-wheel carousel—headstands and gymnastics, head skimming the cranberry-scum floor. Fanny pack Sharpied with crosses, gold chain hooped from earring to lip.

Someone is buying M&Ms for a quarter; someone is buying a quarter stall to stall in the ladies', nails grazing palms. Another fellow tries psalms with Anna, ordering eight two-dollar drinks. Another with Dead-Panna, who does this for tips and then drifts.

All of this is happening and I am an away game, a rival jersey. All of this is happening and home is a province cast off.

Chopped

An ex-boyfriend bounces down the stairs
like a secret ingredient,
naked and asking if the volume can be turned down.

On the screen, competitors sear steak,
purée sweet potatoes, add serranos.
Tension is high.

Two beats pass—enough time to think of a punchline;
decide on seasoning, sweetness, acidity.

Knives sprint through tomatoes
on the chopping board. This is

a black box cooking competition.
At the base of the stairs, an elephant trunk
noses for peanuts.

The dishes get plated
with fifteen seconds left on the clock:

ready for the palate
of a judge, we
cut to commercial.

Families, Subfamilies

Sometimes, all I see is the glance of licorice-ball eye or roof-sharpened claw—squirrel tail disappearing like a spaghetti noodle into the open mouth of an eave.

Other times, they scale the stucco walls, bearing grey backs and eel shocks of white at the belly; play a game of musical chairs where we are the music, stopping; straddle the fire escape; track the scent of burials in the yard.

As winter ends, they make external cheeks of our cupboards: stores of nuts, seeds, bread; in the spring, a Swiss Family Robinson of the attic's pink batting insulation—hairless, shut-eyed babies carried in their mother's mouths.

I'll invite them downstairs for a family feast one rain-plump after-noon, saying, *You might as well,* offering the warmth of walnuts toast-ing in the oven—opening the door, smiling as if I won't shut it when they're all tucked in.

Rhyming Couplet

Shortly after I have given my friend some relationship advice, she is advising me about making a living. *You are a rhyming couplet,* was what I said to her, and she said, *Thank you,* but I didn't think it was the type of thing to be thankful for. *Write about vampires,* was what she said next, and, *It should star Anne Hathaway. Oh, and the one who was a hobbit.* She was kidding but I told her the hobbit one already happened. *We watched that one together,* I said. *I think I watched that one with Brandon,* she said. *Oh god he has nice teeth.*

What that relationship needs is a dentist, I thought but didn't say. It needs an excision. Instead I said, *He whitens, doesn't he? He must.* My friend, she has good strong teeth. They should have a grip on the earth more like the hobbit's feet.

Part of anyone

can see how reasonable it is to stay at home and never leave, because
you've anointed that wall, this toilet, as safe and you'd know it even
if the lights never came back on. Sure thing. For some, the comfort
of eating only pizza every meal, or maybe nothing but knuckle sand-
wiches. The same stomach ache every day. For some, doorjambs are
the rough xylophone at the edge of the highway, the warning you're
straying too far. Any of us could understand this feeling.

His father's squat stature

passed down through his hands,
gesturing as he made conversation at my mother's
Christmas dinner. He spoke of conspiracy
theories as the melon of his breath ripened with wine.

Thanksgiving several years before, we were sent to the IGA
for pumpkin pie. My cheeks were nectarines
bruised wide from dental surgery.
I followed shoppers' eyes from his hands
to my face, his hands to my face, and then we laughed
in the car.

I used to watch his squat hands on the neck and body
of his mandolin. I did not like to see
those breakfast-sausage fingers press the strings,
but I like the silence less now.

A certain amount of bruising might make
a relationship sweeter. Too much,
and my eyes moved from his hands to his face
and back to his hands.

Godwits

We scatter our *love you*s like rice at a wedding, not thinking of the limits of expansion. We read about a bird that fattens itself, absorbs a quarter of its own liver and kidneys on its non-stop flight from Alaska to New Zealand.

Meanwhile, we're watching a marathon special of the celebrity chef cooking show. We are ordering the meat lover's and they know our address. We love the celebrity chef, want to reach out and touch glistening lips, bellies full to bursting.

We want to fast in flight, eventually—we're prepared for something special someday calling. Our love is fat-soluble. It crystallizes into stones.

You can put your fingers on the feelings

like you can put your fingers into the cake or the peanut butter, when no one is looking. Or like when the light's on in your kitchen at night, so you can't see anyone looking if, in fact, they are.

Once your fingers are on the feelings, you may not be able to scoop them like ice cream. Instead you may ask yourself, *Why have I put these here?* If you can get at the feeling, it might taste like over-salted olives, or a cereal past its due date.

Press a feeling and the lid of the garbage can may click open. Press a feeling and there may be two mouths lidded open, each spined and stubborn. Each mawing for something remembered, something anticipated.

Canoodlers

Two people sat nose to nose. Gossip columnists call this canoodling, which means intimacy that is fresh, thin, easy to break. Like stalks of asparagus banded together at an outdoor market.

The canoodlers shared a booth at Buffalo Bill's in Whistler. I tell this to my friend and she says, *Oh, no, nothing can be named that after you've seen* Silence of the Lambs. I have to be reminded: Buffalo Bill is the one who makes himself a woman by sewing a second skin, a leather dress of other women.

I don't tell her that I ran my tongue along the edge of those two together, testing for tenderness first in girl, then boy.

Waffle Cones, 99¢

First, there are cumulus clouds
full as milk-filled breasts. Next,
a confetti of napkins
strewn like petals
down an aisle. Then

he knows the woman scooping
ice cream. I introduce myself
to the bear claw stuck
in the down of her forearm. Outside,

he chooses a spot
near the river. We sit
with our feet on the bench, tongues
lapping. The shadow of an oak tree
sways on his shorts.

Nobody should break up
at this picnic table. As soon

as he's done his ice cream,
I'll do it.

I watch his feet and feed the pigeons,
landing bits of cone under their beaks.

Birthday Tarot

As a ring of people watch, Anna reads my birthday tarot. *Wow, she says, lots of major arcana.* She points to a card called the Emperor at the apex of the Λ. *He's a bit of a patriarch, rule-the-roost typa guy.* The reading says I am blocking change—that I need to stop texting my friend/crush because there's someone new in my life, a pentacle challenge. I am to ditch the Knave for the King.

A knock at the door, the party interloping for a minute before the ring closes back up, the discussion returning to the Emperor, to the blocked femininity of a transposed moon. I call bullshit—can't the Emperor be me? *No, Anna says, this is not sex & gender class. This is you need to get fucked.*

My loyal cabal

of women ask what kind of man will be worthy. Ben rolls his eyes. *Worthy of what?* I am thinking. Maybe Ben is thinking, *This is not an epic. This is not Greek tragedy. What kind of poetry are we writing here?*

I'm not shooting arrows through hoops. Not about to turn into a tree. No. I am bending over and rubbing the hair on my shins. I am humming Kate Bush, getting ready for a run.

The ideal poem

is not at eye level in the sushi display at the supermarket. It's not at the end of a cul-de-sac, forwarding your mail to the wrong address. The man on the corner—the one whose dentures slip down as he talks— he's not holding it out to you in the form of a tri-fold pamphlet. It's not in the spider plant, evangelizing shoots as the sun passes from blinding to mid-sky diffuse, or in the halal butcher's saw, mouthing vowels—*ee-oh-ee*—across the alley.

Your five o'clock,

Ben, maybe your four. Hunched over like we're sharing Frank O'Hara's family secrets. Ben cranes at two—no, three—IT kids in post-work dress-down. Everything so tight, so pinched, stiff as the drinks I had last time I was here. When Ben rolls back, I tell him life's hard for people who think about things. Or it's easy, because you think No, not this sweater. Yes, do unbraid your brow. Count to three and drop your shoulders like a cookie onto a sheet. We're not writing haiku. Everyone here breathes stets, will transpose a word as sure as they'll stir or shake.

Ben and Kim want a sex poem.

Don't sleep with one of your friends though, they say. So I think of the
time I walked thirty blocks south from my house to meet a man with
a froth of dark curls. He smelled like pot and Old Spice, rain settled
into an overcoat. Put his hand on my neck, asked me if I liked it. Took
it off when I said, *No, not really.* Watched me pull a dress over thighs,
up stomach and, hands crossed into armpits, over my head. Traced
the lace of the turquoise bra I'd put on earlier for a failed date—first
with his finger and then with his tongue. *Yes,* he said. *Shit.* Afterwards,
he asked if I wanted to smoke a joint—if it was okay if he did any-
ways. *Do you want me to call you?* he said. *It was nice to meet you,* I said.
No, I said.

There's something missing from the middle, Kim says. *Yes,* says Ben. *The
sex.*

So You're One of Those People Who Thinks They Can
   Control Themselves

Only you're not. You're a room full of servers and the cooling system
has broken down. There are so many cables. You set up these cables.
There should be a map of them in your head. But no, there's a map
of snakes instead. And the room is growing hot and moist from the
greenhouse of your breath.

You're a room full of servers and there are hungry people waiting. All
you can do is watch the chits. Oh, that steak won't cook any faster, as
hard as you watch. As hard as you wait to season it with the sweat, the
hardworking sweat off your hardworking brow.

The bare legs of Toronto

pass each other by, knobby knees nodding from miniskirts and Daisy Dukes. The legs, the arms, the thumbs scrolling, hovering, lighting and pocketing. The tanned skin of Toronto, all of it going somewhere, the thigh-smacks sent like *xoxo*—the exposed shoulders, collarbones, armpits, the chatter and shush. Comfort a possession of beachy thighs, uncombed eyebrows, scuffed and sockless slip-ons. The bare legs demure, peacocked as your best brand ambassador.

These are the park years

of your life. The flouncy, the jersey dress, the barefoot-in-the-bath-room years. The years when you forget the blanket but remember to stop for mini carrots and avocado hummus and chocolate-covered anything. Partially shady, partially reclined years.

Bikes leaning against a walnut tree. A squirrel working a walnut shell. (A hamster wheel, turning, its small attendant noises.) Don't think too much.

Don't think too much: these years are for doing. Doing can mean sleeping under the walnut tree, under the watch of a creature whose teeth never stop growing.

The park bathroom will keep you honest during these years. The condensation on the pipe, on the eye-level lever. Outside, muffled, a person throwing a ball for a dog. Chuckit! arching like a math problem.

Maybe you should cut your shorts a little shorter, run them through the washer a few times too many. Think about this. Don't think, running your hands over the pebbly wall, about how many times this bathroom has been painted over, tagged, painted over again.

Booze is too cheap in Portland,

and I wake remembering a dream—a recurring dream, one I've dreamt in beds across Canada. Later, in the car back to Vancouver, Vonno snores. Her head titled back, mouth open.

In the dream, I am twenty-two or twenty-three. Someone else is driving and the windshield shatters. Sitting in the middle of the back seat, I am crushed by the telephone pole that shatters the windshield.

I can feel it in my core—the muscle memory of something that never happened.

Next to Vonno snoring—in the back seat, next to Vonno snoring—I feel suddenly safe. I'm twenty-six, and I've passed the age at which I should have died.

ΛΛΛ

On the drive back down from the mountain, lesbian fraternity lambda lambda lambda discusses long hairs and short hairs. We are two long hairs, two short hairs and two dogs. Short hairs, I learn, carry the stuff. They fix the shelf and they stand taller, or *like* taller, beside the long hairs. Long hairs can be butch, but they must also use conditioner. The dogs sit between two long hairs in the backseat, clinking teeth and pawing at each other out of obligation. It's conceded: long hairs can date long hairs, yes. But who's going to carry the stuff?

The other short hair is driving: the two of us, long-legged, leg the length of the front seat. *Who should drive?* was asked earlier, and the other short hair and I looked at each other, gearing up, passing keys from hand to hand. Now the dogs sigh and shift, look for thighs to rest their chins on. Hmm, I think, and roll the window down. My scapulae come together, nose to nose, and I think hmm, I think oh—the chins of friends and lovers, chinning the dip of a clavicle.

Listen,

I say to Vonno, reading it all aloud—the messages I sent him late last night. All twelve of them. It gets easier after he stops replying. I no longer need to identify the speaker.

She asks me where she was when this was happening—she and I *did* leave the party together. I tell her she was offering to kill me to prove her love for Oopey. (Oopey was buying pizza, I say.) Vonno remembers the pizza.

I remember showing up at the party. Twenty-sixer of vodka for me and Vonno, a little bottle of bitters. In the front room, a closed circle of close friends. He moved to the couch, made room for me and both of my drinks.

We talked and I don't even remember what about. Him cross-legged, his knee resting on my leg. And then his ex-girlfriend joined the party. Sat right in front of us. Spoke only to me.

This is the part when I flash back to Vonno tipping the bottle upside down, asking, *Where'd it all go?* He'd already left for another part of the room.

And then he said, *Vonno needs to go home, eh?* And his ex-girlfriend left with us, lives in a nearby part of town. Standing next to her, waiting for Vonno and Oopey to eat their pizza, I messaged him. *Got DR NK. Wish I talked to you more.* Eleven more things to follow.

Telling Vonno, she says, *I'm such a bad friend!* Me, I'm scrolling through our conversation again, again, again. It's always me there at the end. Saying, *Hey.* Asking if he's still awake.

Monday,

I walked for a while before catching the bus.
Needed to do some reading. Flipped the pages, scanned
the first few lines—all I could think of was him,
pulling on his bike shoes. Sliding the tongue
into the latch. The click
of the pen under my thumb.

Had some reading to do. Stood firm
against the movement of the bus.

Pen in hand, eyes on the page.
Bus rounded the corner at Dunbar—should've
known it would—
all I could think of was him as I lost
my footing, body-slammed the rear doors.
Gave a good *Jesus fuck!* to the crowded bus, then
a sorry. *Sorry.*

The geoduck of my fever dream

had a lot to share
about sticking its neck out.

We spoke in the aisle of a grocery
that sold seafood and mushrooms—blooming
fungi, ridged shells, the smell of salt and earth.

The cashier asking why I came every day, why
I always paid with cash.

He could have had a lot to say
about sticking his neck out. I could have
tasted his salt and earth.

Instead, we went unsated. Him, an aisle to wander. Me,
a fever dreamer.

Crow comes through

your oven vent for a quick roost, a dust bath in the crumbs of the pie cooling on your counter. Beak deep in the red-purple San Andreas of your kitchen counter. Eyes like a tooth-crack chunk of brown sugar, thickened up with cornstarch. Wingspan the size of a cutlery drawer. Glossy like it's got a budget.

If you were a stick,

what would I fashion you into?

(The Lillooet a rheumy blue eye, whitecapping
down the valley.)

If I held you in my beak,
could I tightrope these rapids?

Would it be different in the spring
than it is in the fall—
melt fleshing the banks,
bears shucking their furlough.

What would you be
if you were not a stick at all?

If I had a beak,

we'd have a neighbourhood. A roost, a rookery in the east; in the
west, this block, these streets, curbs, runways of crab or turf.

If I had feathers, I wouldn't need a haircut. If I had feathers, I'd bathe
in the unseeded dust.

If the water got low, I'd have a rock pile. If I had a beak, I wouldn't
need hands.

If I had a gullet, I'd grind that.

If I had a worm, its meat would be plush as sausage. If I had a
problem, I'd pluck its eyes out.

If you had a wire, it'd be my perch. If you had a tree, it'd be my perch.
A porch? An eave? A roof, a parking sign, a storage pod. Mine.

If you took this house, I'd join you. If the people got too comfortable,
we'd dive-bomb their skylights. If they got a dog, we'd land on
its back.

If you were a crow, I'd be a crow too. And then, when we got
together, it'd be murder.

Blackberries

Well, for a while it was like fresh warm blackberries halving at your two front teeth—the centre a hull with cochlear hairs. You'd eat both halves together, sweet or sour, syrupy or juicy from so much rain. D'you know what I mean? And it wasn't so much like one day there was a worm, maybe just that you'd plop the whole thing into your mouth, not feel the little hairs on your tongue anymore. You'd just shove 'em into your mouth, right to the back, handfuls at a time like the season was ending and you had no choice.

In Seattle,

Lambda lambda lambda stays at the Moore Hotel and the windows open out above the streets. The sills are wide enough to sit for a while, legs *L*'d out like a common Tetris object.

That comes later. First, there's the beer, nested with ice in the sink. This is a goodbye les frat send-off, and our Vonno is leaving for Albuquerque. Is the object the leaving? Or the gimlets, the Slim Jims, the part where we take over the town? The corgi at the third bar, the woman whose nickname is Linebacker.

I am thinking of tri-lamb bifurcation, of how we all want dogs. I am thinking of the Lions, of Grouse and Seymour, Baker and Rainier. How it's thirty degrees down here and the peaks are still covered with snow. Rainier is the farthest south we'll follow Vonno, who will pass St. Helen's and then what? The Corolla dragging down the I-5. Tweeted missives, kilometre tolls.

First we'll all go weird and close the bar and leave the corgi. Vonno will unwrap tubes of meat and she and the other Andrea will whip each other until there's a snap, and how did Hot Nikki cross the table so fast? A Slim Jim Lady-and-the-Tramped between two sets of eye teeth; the inner circle of lambda lambda lambda clutching and laughing and clutching our chests at the metaphor of it all.

First, I'll sit on the wide windowsill and Nikki'll have a nightcap and we'll talk about being in therapy while Vonno sleeps and the other Andrea sleeps and the cars and people pass each other on the street below, like no one cares and everyone has a new place to be.

In the morning, we'll have breakfast and UPS Vonno's bike. In the morning, we'll watch Vonno finish packing. She and the other Andrea will get into the Corolla and Nikki and I will get into the truck and we'll follow the avenue until the signs for the I-5 S and the I-5 N split and then we'll honk and open our throats for as long as possible, until it's not possible anymore.

Acknowledgements

I am so grateful for the feedback, collaboration and love of my UBC Creative Writing colleagues and mentors, in particular Keith Maillard, Rhea Tregebov, Kim Fu, Ben Rawluk, Emily Davidson and Natalie Thompson, who have so often been my first ears and eyes. Thank you, also, to my partner Will Keats-Osborn, who read an early version of the manuscript in an early version of our relationship, and my family, including my brother, who has flown me home to visit more than a couple times in return for the promise that I never, ever write about him, and my dad, who is probably somewhat responsible for many of the poet-y things in my nature.

Poems from this manuscript have previously appeared in the literary journals *Grain, Geist, CV2, Canadian Literature* and *Matrix*, and the anthologies *iLit* from McGraw-Hill Ryerson and *Alive at the Center* from Ooligan Press.

I gratefully acknowledge the financial support of the Social Science and Humanities Research Council (SSHRC) in the form of a Joseph Armand Bombardier Scholarship, which supported the research and writing of this book.

About the Author

andrea bennett's writing has appeared in several literary journals and magazines across North America; her poetry has been anthologized in books from McGraw-Hill Ryerson and Ooligan Press. In 2013, she received a National Magazine Awards honourable mention in the Politics and Public Interest category. She is a contributing editor at *Geist*, and a former editor at *Adbusters*, *This* magazine and *PRISM international*. Originally from Hamilton, andrea now lives in Vancouver with her partner, Will. She is a graduate of the University of British Columbia's MFA program in Creative Writing.

PHOTO CREDIT: TENILLE CAMPBELL